Bossy the Bunny
At Easter

Pamela Griffiths

Published 2018

ISBN-10: 198409548X
ISBN-13: 978-1984095480

Classification: Children's Rhyming Story

Website pamelagriffiths.com
Twitter @pamg50
Facebook Author Pamela Griffiths page

Bossy the Bunny
At Easter

Bossy the bunny

Was running around

Over the hills and grass

He bound

He looked at the

Many daffodils

That were growing

In the grass and hills

Spring has arrived

It's such a lovely time

The weather is warmer

Everything is fine

Bossy was happy

He hopped up and down

His fur was very shiny

A lovely dark brown

He called to his friends

And told them today

Things must be done

The Bossy Bunny way

Bossy the bunny

Told everyone there

He was the boss

So they must take care

He would lead them

And show them how

Bossy needed their help

And he needed it now

'Easter is coming'

'We must hide the eggs'

The bunnies agreed

As they flexed their legs

A pile of eggs

All ready to hide

Were already waiting

With treats inside

Many chocolate Easter eggs

Some large and some small

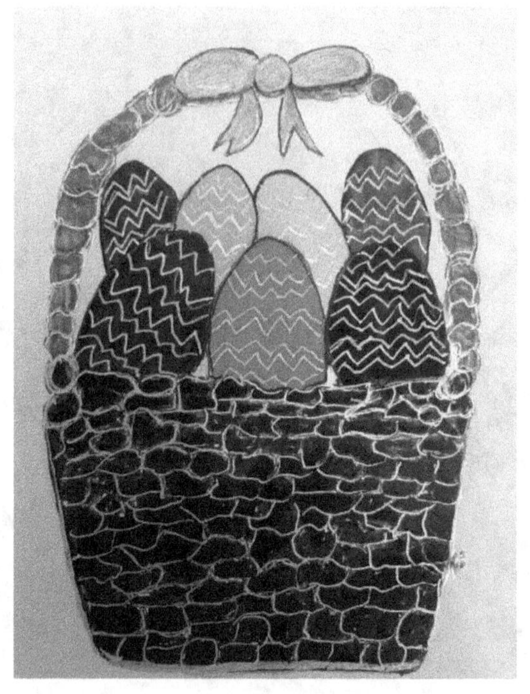

The bunnies have a challenge

To try and hide them all

The children's Easter holiday

Depended on them

The bunnies hide the eggs

So children find them again

Bossy the bunny

Knew he was the one

To organise this Easter

And to get things done

There are so many eggs

To spread all around

They had to go and hide them

So that they could be found

Bossy would need the help

Of all of the others

He would now have to lead

All his sisters and brothers

'Easter is coming'

'We really need to rush'

Bossy tells the bunnies

As they hide eggs in a bush

'Spread the word my friends'

'Tell all your pals"

'The Easter hunt is soon'

'For the little boys and gals'

Lots of lovely Easter eggs

Are being hidden all over

Under stones and hedges

And in the deep clover

Bossy the bunny

Was feeling happy he was glad

His job was almost done

It hadn't been so bad

He was very lucky

The bunnies had been there

They had helped him hide the eggs

Now the eggs were everywhere

'Thank you all so very much'

'I needed your assistance'

'I couldn't have done it on my own'

'We have covered a great distance'

Easter had arrived

The children laughed and found

Lots of lovely Easter eggs

Were hidden all around

'This is a success my friends'

'We have our Easter bunny ears'

'Now we can return again'

'For many more Easter years'

Bossy Bunny is a leader

He always gets things done

But that doesn't mean

They couldn't have some fun

'I love you all my friends'

Bossy bunny said aloud

'Look the children are so happy

'And I'm so very proud'

Good friends help each other

It pays to be kind

Bossy the bunny knows this

So he's always fair you'll find

So Easter is over now

A job has been well done

Bossy bunny and his friends

Have made this Easter so much fun

Happy Easter

The End

Dedication

For my partner Sandy Hoffman
And my family and friends

For the children who have enjoyed this
story and the adults who have enjoyed reading
this book to them.

Thank you

Pamela Griffiths

For more information about Sheffield author
Pamela Griffiths
(National Award winning poet and author)

Please check out these sites.

Website www.pamelagriffiths.com

Twitter (@pamg56) https://twitter.com/Pamg56

Facebook Author page
https://m.facebook.com/Author-Pamela-Griffiths-
167707173288865/

Amazon.co.uk
https://www.amazon.co.uk/Pamela-
Griffiths/e/B0034ODJVQ/ref=ntt_dp_epwbk_0

www.ingramcontent.com/pod-product-compliance
Lightning Source LLC
Chambersburg PA
CBHW071020260726
48662CB00022B/960